Contents

Abstract

Health Care in Mexico: Is U.S. Partnership/Intervention an Advisable Course of Action

Mexico's leadership finds itself confronted with a variety of thorny governance issues including immigration, drug trafficking and education. Alongside these seemingly unsolvable problems sits the issue of health care which is primarily a good news story. The Mexican government has always taken a paternalistic approach to health care to the extent that access to care is a constitutional right. Nationally, Mexico's medical industry has demonstrated the ability to provide a quality of care on par with global leaders, but there are inequities in quality and availability of care as one dissects matters socioeconomically and geographically. This paper looks at the practicality of U.S. partnership with the government of Mexico in tackling these perceived inequities against a backdrop of competing priorities. Finally, the paper concludes with a recommended course of action that not only addresses health care delivery, but also is compatible with complementary security and stability efforts.

INTRODUCTION

Opening Remarks and Thesis

A matter of significance and influence to every responsible government is the health and medical care of its citizenry. Clearly some governments are more concerned, compassionate and responsive than others, but it is a weighty topic of consideration for all administrations nonetheless. The government of the United Mexican States has long placed a premium on the management and delivery of its health care system. Statistical analysis of key health care metrics demonstrates that Mexico is clearly trending in a positive direction in caring for its population. That is not to say that everything is perfect, and that the Mexican people could not benefit from new initiatives or systemic improvements. People in outlying rural areas and the unemployed in particular are receiving lesser care than their urban, working counterparts. More on the particulars of the system will be discussed in the main body of the paper.

The United States, Mexico's neighbor to the north, clearly has a stake in promoting stability in the world and especially on the North American continent. That being said, however, this paper's assertion is that the United States' most advisable course of action is not to undertake any substantive initiatives in the realm of Mexican health care reform or improvement. That position takes into consideration the gamut of big picture issues both in Mexico and the United States. It does not simply consider the state of health care in a vacuum. The primary supporting reasons for this position include the previously stated positive trend in Mexico's current medical/health care scheme of action, the tenuous financial situation that currently exists in the U.S. and the fact that the U.S. has not clearly established adequate credibility in developing and administering its own domestic health care system.

1

DISCUSSION

Setting the Scene

Before exploring these arguments, this section sets out to address the first portion of the assigned research question – *analyze the Mexican health care system nationally and by state to include the policies that the GOM has to ensure a basic level of life sustaining support.*

Generally speaking, the Mexican government takes a more socialistic or at least paternalistic view of health care than does the U.S. In contrast to the United States, access to health care is an actual right bestowed upon all Mexican citizens. The Mexican Constitution articulates this entitlement. Specifically, Article 4 of the Constitution "grants all people protection to their health, a right to housing and rights for children." The Secretariat of Health is the government agency charged with oversight on the matter. Operating under authority of the Secretariat of Health, the Mexican Social Security Institute (IMSS) is the organization charged with administration of public health. Without delving too deeply into a Mexican civics lesson, the IMSS's legal mandate stems from Article 123 of the constitution, and Article 2 of the Social Security Law (SSL) further articulates the guaranteed right to health and medical assistance.[1]

The current health care concept employed by Mexico is not a "one size fits all" scheme. It is a complex, multi-tiered system with two nationally sponsored insurance programs for the employed portion of the Mexican population. Government employees and elite white collar workers have access to private coverage and the best facilities while the middle and lower tiers of the employed population enjoy a lesser degree of coverage and

---

[1] Instituto Mexicano del Seguro Social, Last modified on July 15, 2011, http://www.imss.gob.mx/en/institute.html (accessed 4 September 2011).

access.[2] The IMSS, by its SSL mandate, serves as both an insurer and medical provider.[3] It is the insurer of employed citizens who work for private companies. The other national insurer is the State's Employees' Social Security and Social Services Institute (ISSSTE) which covers all government employees.[4] Both the IMSS and the ISSSTE operate their own facilities and manage the medical providers and staff employed there.

The IMSS and ISSSTE cover the employed segment of the population, but many Mexicans are unemployed or self-employed outside the coverage sphere of the two social security agencies. To address the needs of this sizable constituency, the Mexican government established the System for the Social Protection in Health (SPSS). The SPSS is funded jointly by national and state governments and is endeavoring to expand its reach to the entire Mexican population by 2012 beginning with the poorest families.[5] The continued expansion of SPSS is further evidence of Mexico's commitment to fulfilling its constitutional intent of caring for its people. The drive toward universal coverage is not without its pitfalls and criticisms. Estimates suggest that enrollments are on track to effectively reach full national coverage before the end of 2011, at least on paper. Skeptics question whether the actual care will be forthcoming. The stories of those who have been helped to date under the

---

[2] Eleanor Kinney, "Health Care Financing and Delivery in the United States, Mexico, and Canada: Establishing Intentional Principles for Sound Integration," *Wisconsin International Law Journal*, http:// hosted.law.wisc.edu /wilj/issues/26/3/kinney.pdf, 948 (accessed 4 September 2011).

[3] Instituto Mexicano del Seguro Social, Last modified on July 15, 2011, http:// www.imss.gob.mx/en/institute. html (accessed 4 September 2011).

[4] Instituto de Seguridad y Servicios Sociales de los Trabajadores del Estado, Last modified on August 12, 2011, http://www.issste.gob.mx/english.html (accessed 4 September 2011).

[5] Eleanor Kinney, "Health Care Financing and Delivery in the United States, Mexico, and Canada: Establishing Intentional Principles for Sound Integration," *Wisconsin International Law Journal*, http://hosted.law.wisc.edu /wilj/issues/26/3/kinney.pdf, 952 (accessed 4 September 2011).

plan are heartwarming, but the $12 billion allocated for the plan is likely to be less than adequate.[6]

Another point of concern is the way the funds are designed to flow. Funds go from federal to state governments based on enrollment, and the states then have total discretion on spending. In other words, there is incentive to register as many people as possible, but there is no accountability or oversight.[7]

The scene would not be properly set without a few numbers. As a percent of Gross Domestic Product, Mexico allocates 6.4% in comparison with the U.S which allocates 17.6%.[8,9] Not too much should be read into the raw numbers. The United States spends well above the global norm, while Mexico's percentage outlay is comparable to Canada's health care spending. Infant mortality rates in the wealthier municipalities are on average nine death deaths per thousand births while the number slightly exceeds 100 per 1,000 in the poorest regions.[10] The national figure ends up being approximately 18.8 per 1,000 when combined. The corresponding national figures for the United States and Canada are 6.8 and 5.3 respectively.[11] At the point where Mexico is focusing its greatest attention and resources, wealthier urban areas, quality of care and results approximate its North American neighbors. This is the result of several decades of concerted effort and true commitment to caring for its

---

[6] Elisabeth Malkin, "Mexico's Universal Health Care is Work in Progress," *New York Times*, January 29, 2011, http://www.nytimes.com/2011/01/30/world/americas/30mexico html?pagewanted=2&_r=1&sq=mexicohealthca re&st=cse&scp=1(accessed 4 September 2011).

[7] Ibid.

[8] Eleanor Kinney, "Health Care Financing and Delivery in the United States, Mexico, and Canada: Establishing Intentional Principles for Sound Integration," *Wisconsin International Law Journal*, http:// hosted.law.wisc.edu /wilj/issues/26/3/kinney.pdf, 957 (accessed 4 September 2011).

[9] U.S. Department of Health & Human Services. *National Health Expenditure Data,* https://www.cms.gov/ NationalHealthExpendData/25_NHE_Fact_sheet.asp (accessed 4 October 2011).

[10] Mariana Barraza-Llorens et al., "Addressing Inequity in Health and Health Care in Mexico," *Health Affairs* 21 no. 3 (2002), http://content healthaffairs.org/content/21/3/47 full (accessed 4 September 2011).

[11] Eleanor Kinney, "Health Care Financing and Delivery in the United States, Mexico, and Canada: Establishing Intentional Principles for Sound Integration," *Wisconsin International Law Journal*, http:// hosted.law.wisc.edu /wilj/issues/26/3/kinney.pdf, 955 (accessed 4 September 2011).

citizens. President Calderon has been a strong proponent of the universal health care push and has shepherded the initiative throughout his term in office. It is clear, however, that the quality of care and facilities is not equally distributed throughout the country. Directing more funds to the initiative is an unlikely option. Mexico is experiencing the same financial difficulties as the U.S. and much of the world, and frankly it has priorities that would trump health care reform. As much as Mexico is committed to advancing health care, issues like drug trafficking and cartel activity come first.[12]

To synopsize the analysis of the Mexican health care situation, there are both positives and negatives to report. On the positive side of the ledger, the government truly cares and is committed to reform. Its medical professionals are well educated and have demonstrated the ability to bring the quality of care up tremendously over the past several decades. However, as one moves down the socioeconomic ladder and out into the poorer, rural municipalities, problems begin to emerge. It is in these areas where opportunity for improvement exists. Within its national means and given its relative and more pressing priorities, Mexico is doing what it can. The subsequent arguments and counterarguments address the advisable and practicality of U.S. involvement in the Mexican health care reform issue.

Argument #1 – We Can't Afford It

The United States currently finds itself in dire financial straits. The economy and the budget crisis dominate the news everyday electronically, via broadcast and in print. Accordingly, we need to be circumspect in how we spend both domestically and in the foreign aid arena. Stating an obvious point, ADM Mike Mullen, recently retired Chairman

---

[12] James O. Finckenauer et al., "Mexico and the United States: Neighbors Confront Drug Trafficking," *National Criminal Justice Reference Service,* https://www.ncjrs.gov/pdffiles1/nij/218561.pdf (accessed 11 September 2011).

of the Joint Chiefs of Staff, told a Naval Academy assembly that, "the biggest threat to the country's security is the growing budget deficit, and all spending must be curtailed.[13] He was referring primarily but not exclusively to military fiscal frugality. The fact of the matter is that the ripple effect of the budget situation is going to be felt across the board. The U.S. Department of State (DOS) has already been affected, and all indications are that it will continue to be hit hard. For example, as part of the negotiations that prevented a U.S. government shutdown in April of this year, DOS took an $8 billion budget reduction which was the largest single cut levied on any given department.[14] One item that Republicans and Democrats appear to agree on is that program slashing across DOS aid agencies is inevitable even in these historical times filled with humanitarian crises and global political uncertainty and instability.

Chairwoman of the House appropriations subcommittee overseeing foreign affairs, Representative Kay Granger, indicated that the budget situation is "forcing a fundamental change in how foreign aid is spent and that lawmakers will need to prioritize spending according to American national security interests and justify those decisions to Americans who are generally skeptical of foreign aid."[15] "Prioritize" and "American national security interest" strike me as the most salient points in that quote. Referring to the 2010 National Security Strategy (NSS) section on "Advancing Top National Security Priorities," focus areas explicitly called out in the document include threat from weapons of mass destruction, acquisition and proliferation of nuclear capability by violent extremists, Iran, North Korea, al-Qa'ida, the cyber domain, Israeli/Palestinian relations, Iraq and rebuilding our economic

---

[13] Earl Kelly, "It Isn't That You Fail, It's How You Get Up," *Annapolis Capital*, September 22, 2011, http://ebird.osd mil/ebfiles/e20110923843904.html (accessed 23 September 2011).

[14] Steven Lee Myers, "Foreign Aid Set to Take a Hit in U.S. Budget Crisis," *New York Times*, October 4, 2011, http://ebird.osd mil/ebfiles/e20111004846118.html (accessed 5 October 2011).

[15] Ibid.

strength.[16] Anecdotal observation of the most frequent and prominent news stories would seem to support those priorities listed in the NSS. Nothing in those named priorities suggests Mexico. That is not to say that the U.S. is not going to expend any foreign aid on Mexico, but the health care issue is certainly going to sit lower in the pecking order when compared to crime and drug related issues and immigration. The latter issues pose a clearer, more pressing threat to American national security interest.

The bottom line is that there will not be funds appropriated to invest in a significant, dedicated program targeting Mexican health care reform. As noble and humanitarian as the issue may be, the U.S. is operating in a severely constrained resource environment, and this will not make the cut.

Argument #2 – Current State and Trend of Mexican Health Care
There is no shortage of academic and political discussion on whether or not Mexico is on its way to becoming a failed state. The Mexican government has not been able to successfully exert its influence over the drug trade in its northern border region. National tax revenue is overly dependent on post-peak, steadily declining oil production. Pemex is responsible for 35% of that revenue.[17] Remittances, a significant portion of Mexico's revenue, are unpredictable and subject to economic fluctuation. These and other problem issues will ultimately determine whether Mexico does or does not "fail" as a state. Amidst these problem issues, however, Mexico's health care system stands out as an imperfect but promising program.

---

[16] The White House, *National Security Strategy,* http://www.whitehouse.gov/sites/default/files/rss_viewer/national_security_strategy.pdf, 4 (accessed 15 October 2011).

[17] Russ Winter, "Mexico Could End Up as a Failed State," *Seeking Alpha,* http://seekingalpha.com/article/255214-mexico-could-end-up-as-a-failed-state (accessed 15 October 2011).

At the end of the scene setting analysis of this paper, some numerical statistics were put forth. Numbers can be illustrative, but they don't always tell the whole story. There is often much to be learned from human, qualitative accounts.

An Ohio University team composed of staff medical professionals and nursing students traveled to Mexico and toured numerous health care facilities, medical and nursing schools and attended a *Nursing Development and Practice Conference*. They also had the opportunity to speak with doctors and nurses of many disciplines. They generally found themselves openly welcomed by their Mexican hosts and had surprisingly unfettered access in the sites they toured. On balance, the team's findings were quite positive in its overall assessment of Mexican health care capabilities and practices.[18]

The following observations are taken from that study. Although the team did have an opportunity to visit one of the elite private clinics, most of their findings come from public facilities. The Mexican cardiovascular-specialized hospitals possess heart transplant and other major surgery capabilities comparable to U.S. counterpart facilities. A cardiologist encountered by the team indicated that he was scheduled to be a keynote speaker at an upcoming cardiovascular conference in the United States. Neonatal intensive care units (NICU) consistently used the same intravenous pumps and equipment as state of the art U.S. hospitals. It was common practice for the hospitals to be organized in their practices and forward looking in emphasizing preventive health care practices rather than treatment after the fact alone. They often demonstrated programs designed to take this knowledge out into the community. Nurses, in particular, were committed to continuing their education. Many had earned baccalaureate degrees and were pursuing further education. The norm was for

[18] David M. Lucas and Sharon Denham, "Mexico and the United States: Comparing Culture, Health Care Services and Nursing Practice," Spotlight on Learning, Ohio University, 2004 (accessed 18 September 2011).

nurses to practice computerized charting for patients, while at the time of the study; many U.S. facilities were still using paper charting. The use of technology overall was a welcome surprise to the team. Their suspicion coming in was that the Mexican facilities would be lagging well behind the U.S. technologically, but that was not the case.

The team did note some practices that were marginal or inadequate. Mexican providers were not always diligent about their use of gloves to the standard that American institutions require. Similarly, many of the Mexican facilities allowed for reuse (without cleaning) of gowns. Infection control and avoidance of contamination drive these rigorous practices in the U.S., and transgressors are subject to disciplinary action and fines. Mexican facilities appeared to be more focused on the medical procedures and less on the associated hygiene practices.

Moving on from the Ohio University study, an increasingly popular phenomenon related to Mexican health care is *medical tourism*. This rapid rise in popularity can be attributed to the increasingly improved quality of care available in Mexico and the relatively low cost of that care.[19] News of the quality and cost status has become common knowledge. I find this medical tourism choice particularly compelling. This is not the government, the medical community or academia attempting to push some self-serving agenda. This is consumers voting with their feet. People are making a choice regarding their own health, and many Americans are looking to Mexico. Large and mid-sized Mexican cities offer the lure of well- trained doctors and first rate facilities at a fraction of the cost. To give an idea of typical costs – a doctor visit may run the patient approximately $25, an overnight stay $35, lab cost costs are roughly one-third of what they might be in the U.S. Also, prescription

---

[19] Jose Marc Castro, "Health Care in Mexico." *EXPATFORUM.COM*, August 8, 2009, http://www.expatforum. com /articles/health/health-care-in-mexico html (accessed 4 September 2011).

drugs manufactured in Mexico typically cost the consumer 50% less than similar drugs in the United States.[20] It would be easy to fill several pages with examples and anecdotal accounts of medical tourism cases. The clientele availing itself of this practice is large and diverse. It comprises retirees from all regions, average citizens from Border States and individual from American cities and states far from Mexico who are still too young to qualify for Medicare. The actual number of Americans using the IMSS system is unclear, but estimated to be well into the thousands.[21]

Argument #2 points out several positives of the Mexican health care system. There is no pretense that the system is perfect and not in need of improvement. The key takeaway is that among the array of problem issues plaguing the government of Mexico, health care is trending well and should be less of a priority for remedial attention internally and from the U.S.

Argument #3 – We Lack Credibility

Given the complexity, cost and overall controversial state of the U.S. health care system, I do not see how the U.S. government could realistically approach the government of Mexico with the necessary level of credibility or expertise to lead in making meaningful reforms.

It has already been pointed out that the U.S. outspends Mexico nearly three to one in terms of health care as a percentage of GDP. Figure 1 clearly illustrates that U.S. spending on health care far outpaces every other country. A hallmark of the U.S. approach to its health care plan is large government investment. The notion of selling the government of Mexico

---

[20] Ibid.

[21] Chris Hawley, "Mexico's health care lures Americans," *USA Today*, September 1, 2009, http://www.usatoday.com/news/world/2009-08-31-mexico-health-care_N htm. (accessed 4 September 2011)

on improvements or modifications that call for increased levels of national spending seems farfetched.

Leading up to the U.S. general election in 2008, the direction of health care in America was a highly debated topic. The current administration set out to pass legislation entitled the Patient Protection and Affordable Care Act (PPACA) and the Health Care and Education Reconciliation Act together commonly referred to as Obamacare. The debate was contentious, and the controversial legislation was passed primarily on party line voting. Since then, it has been mired in the court system all the way up through the U.S. Supreme Court.[22]

In the end, the U.S. health care model is expensive beyond Mexico's capability to emulate. Its planned way forward is controversial, and the outcome of the debate and litigation is uncertain. Also worth mentioning once again is medical tourism. It not only supports argument #2 (quality of Mexican health care); it speaks also to the flaws and shortcomings of the American system. On this matter, the U.S. does not possess the bona fides to step in as a model of reform for Mexico.

COUNTERARGUMENTS

Counterargument #1 – It's Not Our Way

Having argued in favor of a de facto laissez-faire approach for the U.S. toward Mexico and its health care program, there are valid arguments to the contrary that must be examined. Generally speaking, it is not the American way to stand idly by and not participate. Two non-binding and non-specific initiatives, the 2005 Security and Prosperity Partnership of North America (SPP) and the 2009 North American Leaders' Summit,

---

[22] Alexander Bolton, "Lawmakers press Supreme Court for verdict on health care law," *The Hill*, February 2, 2011, http://thehill.com/homenews/administration/141631-lawmakers-press-court-for-verdict (accessed 2 October 2011)

concluded with agreements by the three North American heads of state to increase cooperation and information for the purpose of enhancing security and prosperity on the continent.[23] No concrete agenda was established. No real timetable was agreed upon. At best, they can be characterized as top level intent to engage in mutually beneficial security and economic endeavors should opportunities arise. On balance, the current Mexican system continues to improve, but there are gaps and flaws that are unlikely to be adequately addressed in the foreseeable future. We, therefore, have a situation where lives might be saved or quality of life for thousands of our North American neighbors might be significantly enhanced. As a superpower nation, the world's lone superpower, there arguably exists an implied imperative to intervene. Senator John Kerry wrote an impassioned editorial making the case for the U.S. to demonstrate leadership through foreign aid in spite of the severe budget circumstances. He views it as a pay now or pay later dilemma in which the pay later option is a threat to our national security. He further claims that it is part of the American DNA to get involved citing examples like the Marshall Plan and responses to earthquakes in Pakistan and Haiti.[24]

Beyond the genuinely benevolent and altruistic reasons for intervention, there is an existential, self-preservation element to consider. History shows that global powers, like the U.S. today, rise and fall. The time in the seat of power should be valued, used to spread influence and held for as long as possible, because the successor power is likely to look very different. For the Centre for Research on Globalization, Brent Jessop writes, "In brief, America as the world's premier power does face a narrow window of historical opportunity.

[23] Congressional Research Service, *U.S.-Mexico Economic Relations: Trends, Issues, and Implication*, http://www.fas.org/sgp/crs/row/RL32934.pdf, 10 (accessed 11 September 2011).
[24] John Kerry, "Amid budget crisis, a defense of foreign aid," *The Washington Post*, August 3, 2011, http://www.washingtonpost.com/national/on-leadership/amid-budget-crisis-a-defense-of-foreign-aid/2011/08/03/gIQABVFdrI_story.html (accessed 2 October 2011).

This prospect underlines the urgent need for an American engagement in the world that is deliberately focused on the enhancement of international geopolitical stability."[25] The holes in the Mexican health care system represent an opportunity for the U.S. to demonstrate its presence and exercise influence in a geographic area of importance to both countries.

Counterargument #2 – Security/Stability Implications

Regional security, stability and relationship building are factors that must be contemplated (with cost as a consideration but not necessarily as the driver). Promoting security and stability bolster the case for U.S. intervention. Looking once again to the NSS, there are a number of soft, widely interpretable references that serve as Presidential intent. The document mentions themes such as working to strengthen international institutions, meeting basic needs and strengthening alliances.[26] Applying a reasonable interpretation of those themes, a case can be made that somehow partnering with Mexico on shoring up deficiencies in its health care system meets all three of those themes. Mexico's rural northern regions, for example, represent an area where the GOM has been less successful in delivering a full spectrum of care to its citizens. And as a border region with the U.S., we have a stake in improving the operational environment.

An effective medical partnering effort has the potential to touch many Mexican lives and tell a great story in the process. It may be the type of action best suited to erase or mitigate a measure of the ill-will or distrust toward the U.S. harbored to this day by some Mexicans. They tend to be pragmatic in how they view Americans. Alejandro Moreno writes, "Historical experiences and cultural difference have left a permanent mark on

[25] Brent Jessop, "America's Role as the First, Only, and Last Truly Global Superpower," *Centre for Research on Globalization,* http://www.globalresearch.ca/index.php?context=va&aid=8684 (accessed 11September 2011).

[26] The White House, *National Security Strategy,* http://www.whitehouse.gov/sites/default/files/rss_viewer/national_security_strategy.pdf, 12, 39 & 41 (accessed 15 October 2011).

Mexico's collective consciousness, commonly activating a sense of rejection and distrust. On the other hand, most Mexicans believe that closer ties to the United States benefit them."[27] Much of the distrust can be traced back to the mid 1800's when Mexico lost a huge amount of territory to the U.S. during the Texas Revolution and the Mexican War. The territorial shift likely changed the course of history with respect to which country would become the predominant North American power. The U.S. gained territory and resources (gold, silver, copper, uranium, etc.) that were of immeasurable importance to industrial and economic growth. The loss deeply affected Mexicans and gave birth to a resentment that has been passed down through generations.[28] As we get farther removed in time from the perceived transgression, it may be an easier task to change perceptions. Having even a small American face associated with an initiative that saves Mexican lives or improves quality of life may help turn the tide at least with a young generation that has yet to be influenced by history's lessons.

Security, stability and strengthening alliances are priority issues from the highest levels of leadership. Any opportunity to enhance or advance them should receive serious consideration.

CONCLUSIONS and RECOMMENDATIONS

Reconciling the Dilemma

On one hand, the cold, hard, practical arguments suggest one thing. On the other hand, the high-minded, longer view suggests another. A compelling argument can be made both on behalf and against the U.S. involving itself in some form or fashion in working to

---

[27] Alejandro Moreno, "Trust in North America: Why Do Mexicans Distrust Their Continental Neighbors," *NORTEAMERICA* Year 2, number 2, July-December 2007, http://www.cisan.unam mx/Norteamerica/ pdfs/n04/n0404.pdf, 64 (accessed 18 September 2011).
[28] "Mexican War," Microsoft® Encarta® Online Encyclopedia 2000, http://encarta.msn.com © 1997-2000 Microsoft Corporation. All rights reserved (accessed 4 September 2011).

improve deficiencies in the Mexican health care system. I chose words carefully in the paper's thesis stating that it is not advisable to undertake substantive initiatives with respect to health care in Mexico. The key word in the thesis is "substantive." It allows for flexibility in deciding whether or how to act. A new program or programs carrying a hefty price tag or requiring significant resources is simply unrealistic in the current environment. I have written at length about the dire budget picture confronting the United States government. Countless foreign aid and assistance programs with longstanding histories and priority will be facing deep cuts or elimination. There will be no traction for a new big-time initiative for the budgetary reason alone. Add to that the relatively strong state of the current Mexican health care system and the question marks surrounding U.S. health care, and the prospect of a new program is dead on arrival.

A Modest 3D Solution

Doom and gloom aside, finding some way to assist the Mexican government in making some kind of improvements in its health care system is a laudable notion. Former DOS and USAID official, John Norris, has warned against cutting foreign aid too deeply and returning to an overly inward looking posture. He correctly points out that "every ambassador wants to announce something or preside over a ribbon cutting."[29] If sights are set on some type of modest scale engagement rather than an expensive, "*substantive*" plan, there are certainly some viable courses of action to explore. Within the confines of current funding levels, shrewd NORTHCOM planners, in collaboration with embassy country teams (including the USAID representative), could conceive modest, targeted engagements. This would represent the 3D (Defense/Diplomacy/Development) approach in the classic sense.

---

[29] Steven Lee Myers, "Foreign Aid Set to Take a Hit in U.S. Budget Crisis," *New York Times*, October 4, 2011, http://ebird.osd.mil/ebfiles/e20111004846118.html (accessed 5 October 2011).

The Chief of Mission will have the current knowledge of the government of Mexico's desires and priorities. His team will know specifically what medical and health issues, if any, Mexico wishes to partner on. They will also know the geographic areas where Mexico wishes to focus upon. The USAID representative brings connection to any (medical/health) NGO's that are on the ground in the priority areas. USAID also has a checkbook. And, of course, the military brings to the table superior planning, logistics and medical capabilities. Together, the three D's have the potential to make a material difference in medical and health care areas deemed most important by the government of Mexico.

Examples of the types of engagement I am recommending include medical and dental civic action programs – MEDCAP's and DENTCAP's. I have firsthand experience with these initiatives and their employment with resounding success in the Horn of Africa combined joint operations area (CJOA). The concept would translate very neatly to the poor, rural outlying areas of Mexico where the need to supplement available medical care and capability is most pronounced. No new infrastructure would be required. Small teams could be dispatched to specific regions with a specific purpose for a short period of time – flu shots, eye exam or audiograms for two or three neighboring villages, for example. The MEDCAP is relatively easy to plan, highly agile in its ease of execution and creates immediate and lasting impact on those directly affected. The likely recipients of these engagements are statistically the same people mentioned previously that may be harboring feelings of distrust for the U.S. It is a simple vehicle for partnering with the government of Mexico that delivers a big bang for the buck and strategic communication benefits can be reaped.

It is beyond the scope of this paper to delve too deeply into speculation, but it is reasonable to believe there would be second and third order impacts if medical and health care issues significantly improved. Any engagement we undertake would be a legitimate act in and of itself, but it would also be much more. It would be a vehicle for U.S. presence in a region of interest and value. Any effort the U.S. devotes to the health care delivery potentially frees up resources Mexico can in turn devote to its more pressing issues. As the health care issue stabilizes, it potentially erodes one area of exploitation. Cartels, criminal organizations and any other bad actors would have one fewer grievance to prey upon.

FINAL REMARKS

The research question and the response in this paper should be looked at from two perspectives. Looking specifically and narrowly at the issue of health care, Mexico is engaged and has made real strides over the last several decades. In a severely constrained resource environment, a cost/benefit analysis will dictate where and how Mexico chooses to direct its focus and funding. The chance that health care wins out over other priority issues is slim. The U.S. is also not going to jump in as a large investor in Mexican health care reform. Prevailing circumstances do not allow the luxury of fixing every problem.

Change the optic slightly, and reduce the scale. Rather than viewing this as yet another problem to be solved, the U.S. should view the health care issue in Mexico as a legitimate vehicle to gaining access in support of its own interests.

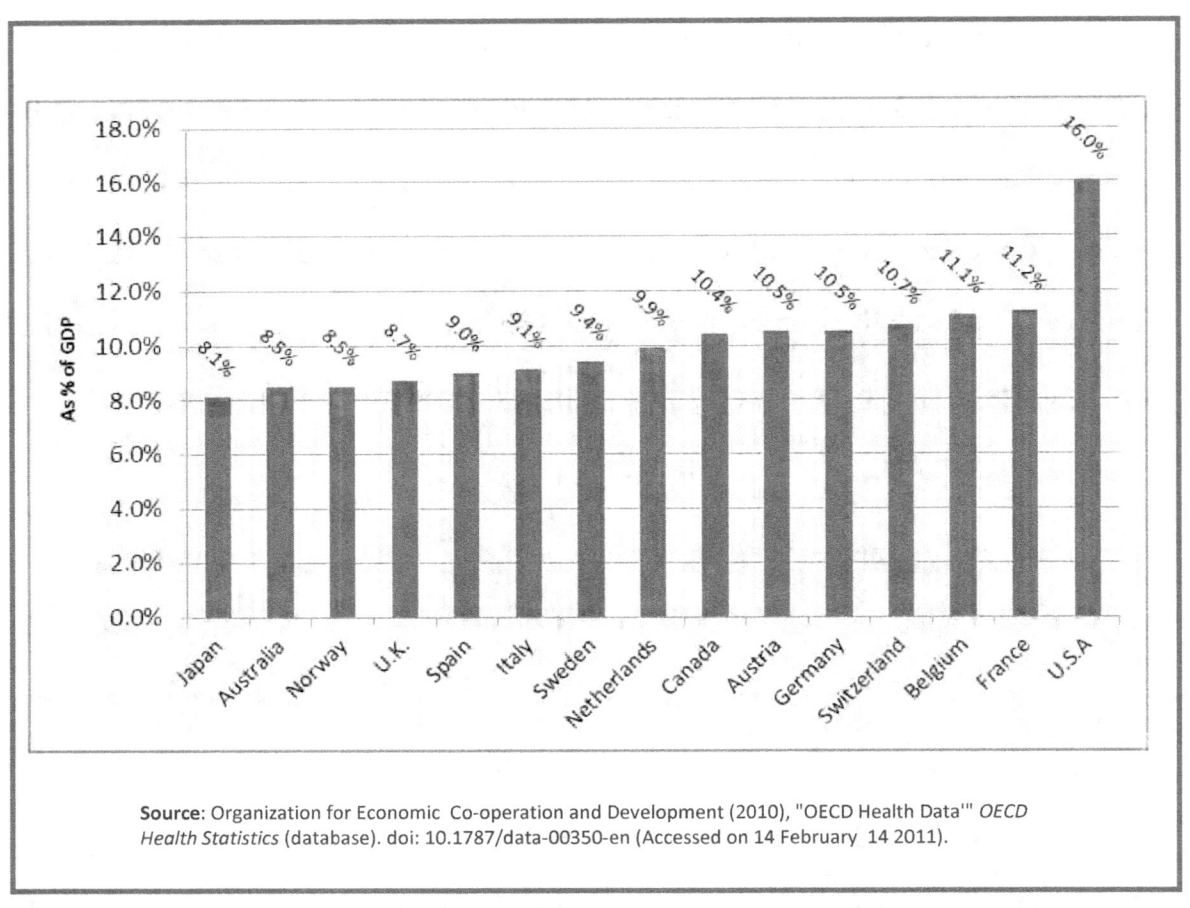

Source: Organization for Economic Co-operation and Development (2010), "OECD Health Data'" *OECD Health Statistics* (database). doi: 10.1787/data-00350-en (Accessed on 14 February 14 2011).

Figure 1

BIBLIOGRAPHY

Barraza-Llorens, Mariana, Stefano Bertozzi, Eduardo Gonzalez-Pier, and Juan Pablo Gutierrez. "Addressing Inequity in Health and Health Care in Mexico." *Health Affairs* 21 no. 3 (2002). http://content.healthaffairs.org/content/21/3/47.full (accessed 4 September 2011).

Bolton, Alexander. "Lawmakers press Supreme Court for verdict on health care law." *The Hill*, February 2, 2011. http://thehill.com/homenews/administration/141631-lawmakers-press-court-for-verdict (accessed 2 October 2011).

Castro, Jose Marc. "Health Care in Mexico." *EXPATFORUM.COM*, August 8, 2009. http://www.expatforum.com/articles/health/health-care-in-mexico.html (accessed 4 September 2011).

Congressional Research Service. *U.S.-Mexico Economic Relations: Trends, Issues, and Implication.* http://www.fas.org/sgp/crs/row/RL32934.pdf (accessed 11 September 2011).

Finckenauer, James O., Joseph R. Fuentes, George L. Ward. "Mexico and the United States: Neighbors Confront Drug Trafficking." *National Criminal Justice Reference Service.* https://www.ncjrs.gov/pdffiles1/nij/218561.pdf (accessed 11 September 2011).

Hawley, Chris. "Mexico's health care lures Americans." *USA Today*, September 1, 2009. http://www.usatoday.com/news/world/2009-08-31-mexico-health-care_N.htm (accessed 4 September 2011).

Instituto de Seguridad y Servicios Sociales de los Trabajadores del Estado. Last modified on August 12, 2011. http://www.issste.gob.mx/english.html (accessed 4 September 2011).

Instituto Mexicano del Seguro Social. Last modified on July 15, 2011. http://www.imss.gob.mx/en/institute.html (accessed 4 September 2011).

Jessop, Brent. "America's Role as the First, Only, and Last Truly Global Superpower." *Centre for Research on Globalization.* http://www.globalresearch.ca/index.php?context=va&aid=8684 (accessed 11 September 2011).

Kelly, Earl. "It Isn't That You Fail, It's How You Get Up." *Annapolis Capital*, September 22, 2011. http://ebird.osd.mil/ebfiles/e20110923843904.html (accessed 23 September 2011).

Kerry, John. "Amid budget crisis, a defense of foreign aid." *The Washington Post*, August 3, 2011. http://www.washingtonpost.com/national/on-leadership/amid-budget-crisis-a-defense-of-foreign-aid/2011/08/03/gIQABVFdrI_story.html (accessed 2 October 2011).

Kinney, Eleanor. "Health Care Financing and Delivery in the United States, Mexico, and Canada: Establishing Intentional Principles for Sound Integration." *Wisconsin International*

Law Journal. http://hosted.law.wisc.edu/wilj/issues/26/3/kinney.pdf (accessed 4 September 2011).

Lucas, David M., and Sharon Denham. "Mexico and the United States: Comparing Culture, Health Care Services and Nursing Practice." Spotlight on Learning, Ohio University, 2004 (accessed 18 September 2011).

Malkin, Elisabeth. "Mexico's Universal Health Care is Work in Progress." *New York Times*, January 29, 2011. http://www.nytimes.com/2011/01/30/world/americas/30mexico.html? pagewanted=2&_r=1&sq=mexicohealthcare&st=cse&scp=1 (accessed 4 September 2011).

"Mexican War." Microsoft® Encarta® Online Encyclopedia 2000. http://encarta.msn.com © 1997-2000 Microsoft Corporation. All rights reserved. (accessed 4 September 2011).

Moreno, Alejandro. "Trust in North America: Why Do Mexicans Distrust Their Continental Neighbors," *NORTEAMERICA* Year 2, number 2, July-December 2007. http://www.cisan.unam.mx/Norteamerica/pdfs/n04/n0404.pdf (accessed 18 September 2011).

Myers, Steven Lee. "Foreign Aid Set to Take a Hit in U.S. Budget Crisis." *New York Times*, October 4, 2011. http://ebird.osd.mil/ebfiles/e20111004846118.html (accessed 5 October 2011).

Richardson, John H., "The Other Public Option: In Search of Better Health Care Abroad." *Esquire*, September 22, 2009. http://www.esquire.com/the-side/richardson-report/mexico-health-care-system-092209#ixzz1Xem3B6TB (accessed 4 September 2011).

The White House. *National Security Strategy*. http://www.whitehouse.gov/sites/default/files/ rss_viewer/national_security_strategy.pdf (accessed 15 October 2011).

Winnefeld, Sandy. "NORTHCOM Commander: Mexico's Struggle is About the Security (Control) of North America." *NORAD and USNORTHCOM Commander's Blog*. February 21, 2011. http://northcom.mil/NNCBlog/2011/02/18/OneofManyTragedies.aspx (accessed 4 September 2011).

Unsigned. "U.S. Northern Command visits Mexico." *NORAD and USNORTHCOM Commander's Blog*. September 16, 2011. http://www.northcom.mil/NNCBlog/2011/09/16/ USNorthernCommandVisitsMexico.aspx (accessed 4 September 2011).

U.S. Department of Health & Human Services. *National Health Expenditure Data*. https://www.cms.gov/NationalHealthExpendData/25_NHE_Fact_sheet.asp (accessed 4 October 2011).

U.S. Department of State. *Background Note: Mexico*. http://www.state.gov/r/pa/ei/bgn/ 35749.htm (accessed 4 September 2011).

Winter, Russ. "Mexico Could End Up as a Failed State." *Seeking Alpha*. http://seekingalpha. com/article/255214-mexico-could-end-up-as-a-failed-state (accessed 15 October 2011).